Harlem
Renaissance

THIS EDITION

Editorial Management by Oriel Square
Produced for DK by WonderLab Group LLC
Jennifer Emmett, Erica Green, Kate Hale, *Founders*

Editor Maya Myers; **Photography Editor** Nicole DiMella; **Managing Editor** Rachel Houghton; **Designers** Project Design Company;
Researcher Michelle Harris; **Copy Editor** Lori Merritt; **Indexer** Connie Binder; **Proofreader** Susan K. Hom;
Sensitivity Reader Ebonye Gussine Wilkins; **Series Reading Specialist** Dr. Jennifer Albro

First American Edition, 2024
Published in the United States by DK Publishing, a division of Penguin Random House LLC
1745 Broadway, 20th Floor, New York, NY 10019

Copyright © 2024 Dorling Kindersley Limited
24 25 26 27 10 9 8 7 6 5 4 3 2 1
001–339804–Jun/2024

A catalog record for this book is available from the Library of Congress.
HC ISBN: 978-07440-9456-5
PB ISBN: 978-07440-9453-4

DK books are available at special discounts when purchased in bulk for sales promotions, premiums, fund-raising, or educational use.
For details, contact:
DK Publishing Special Markets, 1745 Broadway, 20th Floor, New York, NY 10019
SpecialSales@dk.com

Printed and bound in China

www.dk.com

Level

3

Harlem
Renaissance

Melissa H. Mwai

DK

Contents

The Dreamer of Harlem

It was a bright September morning in 1921. A young Black man named Langston Hughes stepped off the subway at 135th Street in Harlem, a neighborhood in New York City. All around him, Black folks were on their way to work. Langston was excited. He wanted to shake hands with everyone who passed by.

Langston was very happy to be living in Harlem. The Jazz Age was in full swing. He had gotten to see the famous singer Florence Mills in *Shuffle Along* at the Cort Theater. It was, he later wrote, "a honey of a show."

The neighborhood was rich with Black art and Black artists. It seemed like a celebration of Black culture was blossoming around every corner.

Langston's dream was to become a famous writer. And he felt sure that Harlem was the place where he could make that dream come true.

Heading to Harlem

In the early 1900s, Harlem was known as the Black capital of America. Like Hughes, many people wanted to be part of the largest Black community in the US.

Many people moved to Harlem for a new beginning. Black people in the US faced unfair treatment because of their skin color. This is known as racism. This was especially true in southern states, where slavery had once been common. Laws separated Black and white people in public. This was called segregation.

The Other Renaissance
From the 14th to the 17th centuries, people in Europe made advances in knowledge, science, and art. This time is known as "the Renaissance."

There was segregation and racism in Harlem, too. However, the supportive community there made life better. Churches and community centers helped newcomers. Black businesses served everyone. Over time, Black life and culture thrived in Harlem.

The time from the end of World War I through the 1930s is known as the Harlem Renaissance [reh-nuh-SAHNTS]. Renaissance means "rebirth." During the Harlem Renaissance, Black people changed their culture in exciting ways.

The History of Harlem

Before there were brick buildings and busy streets, Harlem was farmland. The Lenape people lived and traveled there.

In the 1600s, Dutch settlers claimed this land by "buying" it from the Lenape. The Lenape believed they were sharing the land, but the Dutch believed it now belonged to them. The Dutch named their village Nieuw Haarlem, after a city in the Netherlands. Later, the name changed to Harlem.

Beginning at the end of the 19th century, millions of people immigrated to the US. Many people came to New York City. The city's population exploded. Harlem was less crowded than some parts of the city. So, some immigrants moved there.

But from 1893 to 1896, the American government lost a lot of money. People lost their jobs and homes. Many white people moved out of Harlem. This made room for a new community to grow.

From the 1910s to the 1970s, about six million Black people moved out of the American South. Since the Civil War, life for Black people in the South had been difficult. It was hard for them to get jobs that paid well. In the North, they could build railroads or work in factories. So, many Black people moved to northern cities, like Chicago, Detroit, and New York. This period of movement was called the Great Migration. Many of these people moved to Harlem.

The Migration Series, Panel No. 3, Jacob Lawrence, circa 1940

Unfair Farming

After slavery ended, some laws made it difficult for Black people to own land. Some white landowners rented land or tools to white and Black farmers. The farmers paid the landowners with crops that they grew. This was called sharecropping. Sharecropping deals were often unfair to the farmers. Sometimes it was impossible for farmers to pay what they owed. This made it very hard for the farmers to get out of these arrangements.

Philip A. Payton Jr.
(1876–1917)

One person played a big part in building up the Black community in Harlem. Philip A. Payton Jr. ran rental businesses for white landlords there. He wrote newspaper ads encouraging Black people to rent homes. In 1904, Payton started the Afro-American Realty Company. It helped Black people fight for fair rent prices. It lessened racism against Black renters. Payton became known as "the father of Harlem."

While new Black residents were more welcome in Harlem, the Great Migration was not as well received in other places. And trouble in other places would bring change to Harlem, too.

Philip Payton Jr., Company
Real Estate and Insurance

New Law Apartments, with all improvements; Old Law Apartments, with or without steam heat.   Rents $7 to $30.

We have a number of desirable private houses for Rent or for sale to good tenants.   Rents $60 to $85.

360 EAST 160TH ST.   } 4 and 5 rooms, bath, hot water.   Rent, $17.
840 COURTLANDT AVE.   }   to $19.

Particulars upon request.   67 WEST 134TH ST.

Telephone 917 & 918 Harlem.

Subway Trains

Another reason Harlem became popular was the completion of the subway line to the neighborhood in 1904. For the first time, trains from other places in New York City went to Harlem. People could live in Harlem and work in other parts of the city. The trains were not segregated, and the price of a ticket was the same for everyone.

Changes Coming in Harlem

On July 2, 1917, a series of violent attacks began in East St. Louis, Illinois. Some white people were angry that so many Black people were moving up from the South. They attacked Black workers as they left work for the day. They burned Black people's homes. After a week, about 200 Black people had been killed.

Weeks later and a thousand miles away, nearly 10,000 people joined a silent march in New York City to protest the attacks in East St. Louis. As racial tensions swelled around the country, a new push for freedom began. And Harlem was home to many leaders of the fight.

W. E. B. Du Bois
(1868–1963)

W. E. B. Du Bois was an activist. An activist works to create social change. Du Bois believed Black and white races were equal. He attended an unsegregated high school. He graduated from Harvard University. He wrote about Black and white people living together. He also wrote to protest segregation of the government under President Woodrow Wilson.

NAACP
In 1909, Du Bois helped to create the National Association for the Advancement of Colored People. As it did then, the organization today demands equality for all and fights against injustice everywhere.

Ida B. Wells-Barnett
(1862–1931)

Ida B. Wells-Barnett was an activist and a journalist. She was born in Mississippi to enslaved parents. In 1892, her friend Thomas Moss, a Black man, was killed by a white mob in Memphis. For the rest of her life, Wells-Barnett wrote articles and gave speeches against attacks like this. Wells-Barnett was a founder of the NAACP. In 1913, she also started the Alpha Suffrage Club, a Black women's club supporting voting rights for women.

Mob Attacks

Between the end of the Civil War and 1950, thousands of Black people were killed by white crowds. These attacks happened mostly in southern states.

Marcus Garvey (1887–1940)

Marcus Garvey was raised in Jamaica and educated in London before moving to Harlem. He started a restaurant and a newspaper and helped other Black businesses support themselves. Garvey believed that all Black people should live in Africa. He started the Universal Negro Improvement Association, or UNIA. This group believed in Black pride and unity. Garvey made the phrase "Black is beautiful" popular.

Alain Locke
(1885–1954)

In 1924, the writer Alain Locke talked about "The New Negro." Locke believed that many white Americans wanted to keep Black people from succeeding. But now that slavery had ended, Locke thought that Black writers could and should tell new stories about Black life.

Barbeuce, Archibald Motley, circa 1934

Culture Blooms in Harlem

Black leaders shared ideas to make life better. More people moved to Harlem. And the culture of Harlem bloomed. Many of the people we remember from the Harlem Renaissance were leaders in writing, art, music, and sports.

Writing

In the 1920s and 1930s, newspapers and magazines with Black editors published works by Black writers. Even white-owned newspapers reviewed these popular stories.

Langston Hughes
(1901–1967)

Langston Hughes wrote poetry about the regular lives of Black Americans. His first poem, "The Weary Blues," was published in 1925. In the poem, a man sings about being tired and lonely. People understood how this man felt. They liked the poem. Hughes wrote many poems about people of all ages living in Harlem. No wonder he is called "the people's poet"!

Singing the Blues

Blues music was created after the Civil War by Black Americans. It grew out of work songs and spirituals that used a call-and-response pattern.

Zora Neale Hurston
(1891–1960)

As a little girl in Florida, Zora Neale Hurston loved hearing the people in her town tell stories. When she grew up, she started writing stories of her own. In 1925, she moved to Harlem. She entered a magazine's writing contest and won four prizes. She made friends with Langston Hughes and W. E. B. Du Bois. She collected and wrote stories for the rest of her life.

Hurston's novel *Their Eyes Were Watching God* was published in 1937. In her novel and her stories, Hurston imagined equal rights for women.

Effie Lee Newsome
(1885–1979)

Effie Lee Newsome celebrated the lives of Black children in her poems. Newsome edited a children's column in *The Crisis*, a political magazine that started in Harlem.

Arturo Alfonso Schomburg
(1874–1938)

Arturo Alfonso Schomburg was an Afro–Puerto Rican history writer. He collected books about African history. Today, his collection is part of a research library and museum called the Schomburg Center.

Visual Art

Black artists created many great works of art during the Harlem Renaissance. They were inspired by their African roots, popular music, and people in their community.

Black artists could show their work in many places in Harlem. But there was still racism in the art world. Black artists were often paid less than white artists. In 1935, Harlem artists formed a group to support new artists, host art shows, and fight for better pay.

Harlem Street Scene, Jacob Lawrence, 1942 (detail)

Augusta Savage
(1892–1962)

Augusta Savage was a sculptor. Her sculpture *The Harp* was based on the song "Lift Every Voice and Sing." Millions of people admired *The Harp* at the 1939 World's Fair. Sadly, the plaster sculpture, along with the other art from the fair, was destroyed when the fair was over.

In 1938, Savage started the Harlem Community Art Center to support young Black artists. The center provided free or low-cost arts education.

James Van Der Zee
(1886–1983)

James Van Der Zee took photographs of regular people in Harlem. Van Der Zee wanted the people to look their best. He gave them flowers and fancy costumes to wear. He even drew sparkly jewelry on the photos!

Van Der Zee took pictures of basketball teams, church groups, and military parades. In 1924, he became the photographer for Marcus Garvey's UNIA.

Aaron Douglas
(1899–1979)

Aaron Douglas moved to Harlem in 1925 to make art for magazines. Douglas mixed modern and African art in his paintings. The paintings used bold shapes and bright colors. He was known as "the father of African American art."

Loïs Mailou Jones
(1905–1998)

Loïs Mailou Jones had her first art exhibit when she was 17. She came to Harlem to study art. Her paintings featured African masks with rich colors and patterns. She also illustrated books for Black children.

Folk Musicians (detail),
Romare Bearden, 1942

Romare Bearden
(1911–1988)

Romare Bearden was a
collage artist and painter.
He worked as a social worker in New York
City during the day and painted at night.
His art showed life in the city as well as
scenes from his childhood in the South.
Bearden made many paintings. They
were shown throughout the US and
Europe during his lifetime.

Music and Dance

After World War I, jazz music and dancing became popular in America. This time became known as "the Jazz Age." It played a big part in the Harlem Renaissance. Jazz music was created by Black Americans in New Orleans, Louisiana. As more Black people moved to Harlem, its night clubs became hot spots for jazz.

Changing Times

The energetic spirit of jazz music was new and different. Older people thought jazz music was wild. Young people loved dancing to the fast songs!

Duke Ellington
(1899–1974)

Duke Ellington was a jazz piano player and composer. Ellington led the band at the Cotton Club in Harlem from 1927 to 1931. Recordings and national radio broadcasts of the band's shows made Ellington famous all over the country. He hosted several concerts to raise money for the NAACP. His career lasted for over 50 years.

Club Spotlight

From 1923 to 1935, the Cotton Club was the place to be and be seen in Harlem. Bands played music for people to dance to. The club put on shows with singing, dancing, comedy, and more. Most of the performers were Black. But with very few exceptions, only white customers were allowed at the club.

Bessie Smith
(ca. 1894–1937)

Bessie Smith was known as "the Empress of the Blues." Smith sang about being a Black woman in America. Her first big hit, "Down-Hearted Blues," was recorded in 1923. Audiences liked the way her strong voice told about both good and bad times

Smith recorded 160 songs in her life. She was the highest-paid Black entertainer in Harlem. She sang with other jazz artists, like Louis Armstrong and Sidney Bechet. Smith was inducted into the Rock and Roll Hall of Fame in 1989.

Billie Holiday
(1915–1959)

Billie Holiday was a popular jazz singer in Harlem in the 1930s. Holiday became the first Black woman to sing with an all-white band. Her most famous song, "Strange Fruit," was about the murders of Black people in front of white crowds. Some people think of this as the first American protest song for equal rights. This song sold a million copies, more than any of Holiday's other records.

Josephine Baker
(1906–1975)

Josephine Baker's dancing and costumes made her famous in both Harlem and Paris, France. During World War II, she sang and danced for troops. But the audience didn't know that Baker was a spy. She passed messages written in invisible ink on her music.

Until her death, Baker fought racism. She refused to perform in places where Black and white people couldn't be together. In 1963, she spoke at the March on Washington with Martin Luther King Jr.

Florence Mills
(1896–1927)

Florence Mills was a star of the stage. She sang and danced in musical shows. People of all races rushed to see her in New York City and in Paris. About 150,000 people attended her funeral in Harlem.

James Weldon Johnson
(1871–1938)

James Weldon Johnson was an activist and a writer. He wrote the lyrics for the song "Lift Every Voice and Sing." The song asked Black people to march for freedom. Since the civil rights movement of the 1960s, it has been known as the Black National Anthem.

Sports

After World War I, Americans wanted to forget the war. Playing sports was one way to do that. The 1920s was known as "the Golden Age of Sports" in the US.

At that time, teams, leagues, and championships were segregated. Black players were on Black teams, and white players were on white teams.

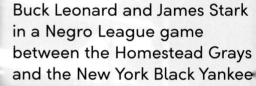

Buck Leonard and James Stark in a Negro League game between the Homestead Grays and the New York Black Yankee

John Henry "Pop" Lloyd (1884–1964)

The Lincoln Stars were a Harlem baseball team. Pop Lloyd was the Stars' best batter and shortstop. In 1913, Lloyd and the Stars won 101 games and lost only six. They beat the Chicago American Giants to win the Negro League championship.

Black vs. White

Black and white teams didn't usually play against each other. But sometimes, they met for extra games. Games between Black and white teams were very popular. Thousands of Black and white fans gathered in the stands to watch. The Stars beat many white teams, including the Philadelphia Phillies, the second-best white team in the country.

VICTORY FIELD
INDIANAPOLIS
FRI. AUG. 31 8:00 P.M.
Adults $1.25   Children 12 & Under 25¢
NEGRO American LEAGUE
BASEBALL
25 TIMES WORLD'S Champions
GOOSE TATUM
KANSAS CITY MONARCHS
VS
HARLEM Stars
SEE IN ACTION—LE ROY "SATCHEL" PAIGE
THE AGELESS WONDER · REPUTEDLY THE
GREATEST PITCHER OF ALL TIME!

Black basketball teams rented out dance floors to play on. The team that played in the Renaissance Ballroom called themselves the Rens. They were the first all-Black, Black-owned professional basketball team in history. Between 1923 and 1947, the Rens won 2,318 games and lost 381.

John Isaacs, also known as Boy Wonder, who signed with the Harlem Rens in 1936

The New York Rens, photographed by James Van Der Zee, 1925

Like the Stars, the Rens defeated many white teams. In 1939, the Rens beat the Oshkosh All-Stars to win the first World Professional Basketball Tournament. The Rens were champions!

Women in the Game

There were Black sports teams for women as well as for men. In 1913, Edith Trice was a leading player on Harlem's Younger Set basketball team. They played their home games at Young's Casino in Harlem.

Fashion

Some people in Harlem used fashion to display their creativity and pride. In the 1920 shorter haircuts and hemlines for women made the news.

Madam C. J. Walker
(1867–1919)

In 1905, Madam C. J. Walker spent $1.25 to start a business. She made hair products for Black women. They became very popular. Walker became the first self-made female millionaire in America.

Walker wanted to improve the lives of Black people. She gave thousands of Black women jobs. She gave money to many organizations that supported Black people.

Ibn al-Haytham

The Man Who Discovered How We See

Libby Romero

NATIONAL
GEOGRAPHIC

Washington, D.C.

For Mom and Dad. Thanks. —L.R.

Trade paperback ISBN: 978-1-4263-2500-7
Reinforced library binding ISBN: 978-1-4263-2501-4
Special sale edition ISBN: 978-1-4263-2616-5

Editor: Shelby Alinsky
Art Director: Callie Broaddus
Editorial: Snapdragon Books
Designer: YAY! Design
Photo Editor: Christina Ascani
Rights Clearance Specialists: Michael Cassady & Mari Robinson
Manufacturing Manager: Rachel Faulise
Producer, 1001 Inventions: Ahmed Salim
Illustrator, 1001 Inventions: Ali Amro

The author and publisher gratefully acknowledge the expert content review of this book led by Professor Mohamed El-Gomati, OBE (University of York) and Professor Salim Al-Hassani (emeritus, University of Manchester) of the Foundation for Science, Technology and Civilisation (United Kingdom), and the literacy review of this book by Mariam Jean Dreher, professor of reading education (University of Maryland, College Park).

The information in this book is based largely on research provided by the exhibit "1001 Inventions and the World of Ibn al-Haytham." The exhibit is a global campaign produced by 1001 Inventions and the King Abdulaziz Center for World Culture in partnership with UNESCO for the International Year of Light 2015. For further information and resources, visit: www.ibnalhaytham.com.

1001 Inventions gratefully acknowledges the support of: Foundation for Science, Technology and Civilisation, Ms. Namira Salim, Shaikh Hisham bin Abdulaziz Al Khalifa, Mr. Naveed Anwar, Kuwait Finance House, Goldfayre Ltd, Almadinah Almunawarah International Academy, Zuhair Fayez Partnership, and those supporters who chose to remain anonymous.

National Geographic supports K–12 educators with ELA Common Core Resources. Visit natgeoed.org/commoncore for more information.

Printed in the United States of America
16/WOR/2

Ann Lowe
(1898–1981)

White-owned stores did not serve Black customers, so Black designers like Ann Lowe opened shops. Lowe designed dresses for all types of women. She designed the wedding dress for future first lady Jackie Kennedy.

Ruby Bailey
(1905–2003)

Ruby Bailey was a dressmaker, painter, and actress. Her family moved from Bermuda to Harlem in 1912. She was famous for patterns and beadwork. Her designs matched the vibrant spirit of Harlem.

Harlem Goes On

The Harlem Renaissance brought a lot of changes. Those changes still affect us today. Organizations like the NAACP and the Schomburg Center are still active in Harlem. More than a century later, they still work to support the lives of Black people everywhere.

Harlem Renaissance leaders planted the seeds for the civil rights movement of the 1950s and 1960s. This was a time when many Americans fought for equal rights for all people. Those same leaders also inspire Black Lives Matter activists today.

Harlem Renaissance artists and athletes paved the way for future stars. They inspired them, too.

The writer Alice Walker made it her mission to make Zora Neale Hurston's work popular again in the 1970s.

Singers like Janis Joplin and Queen Latifah got song ideas from Bessie Smith.

Queen Latifah as Bessie Smith in the movie *Bessie*

Basketball star Kareem Abdul-Jabbar made a film about the Harlem Rens.

Kareem Abdul-Jabbar

A century ago, Harlem was the place to be. The great leaders and stories from the Harlem Renaissance still inspire today's leaders. People everywhere continue to enjoy the art and ideas that came out of the Harlem Renaissance. The Black leaders of this important time broke new ground. Their stories give people in Harlem, and around the world, hope for tomorrow.

Glossary

Activist
A person who works to create social change

Civil rights
Rights that promise equal opportunities and fair treatment for all people regardless of their race, sex, gender, religion, or nationality

Civil War
A war fought in America from 1861 to 1865, between Americans in northern states and Americans in southern states, primarily over the issue of slavery.

Colored
An outdated word for Black people, considered offensive today. It can be used when talking about history or referring to organizations like the National Association for the Advancement of Colored People.

Culture
The beliefs and ways of life of a group of people

Equality
Treatment that is the same for all people

Injustice
Unfair treatment

Jazz
A music form with roots in the American South

Landlord
A person who owns houses and rents them to others

Movement
People working together for a cause they believe in

Negro
An outdated word for Black people which can be considered offensive today. It can be used when talking about history or referring to organizations like the Negro Leagues.

Protest
To express pain, unhappiness, or dissatisfaction about a situation

Racism
Unfair treatment because of one's skin color or race

Roots
The history or origin of a culture, a practice, or a person's family

Sculptor
An artist who makes three-dimensional art

Segregation
Separation of people by their race or skin color

Slavery
The practice of owning people and forcing them to work without pay

Unity
A state of togetherness, particularly in thoughts or ideas

Index

Quiz

Answer the questions to see what you have learned. Check your answers in the key below

1. What does Renaissance mean?

2. How did Philip Payton Jr. help Black people in Harlem?

3. Which Harlem Renaissance writer collected stories?

4. What sports were popular during the Harlem Renaissance?

5. During what two decades did the Harlem Renaissance mostly take place?

1. Rebirth 2. He rented houses to them 3. Zora Neale Hurston
4. Basketball and baseball 5. The 1920s and 1930s

Table of Contents

Who Was Ibn al-Haytham?

Al-Hasan Ibn al-Haytham (al-HAS-un IB-un al-HAY-thum) was an Arab scholar who lived in the 10th and 11th centuries. He was an expert in science and math. He made important discoveries about light and about the way vision works. He also used a new way to study science that scientists still use today.

Ibn al-Haytham was one of the great thinkers of his time. Since then, his ideas have helped other scientists make new discoveries of their own. Many people think he was one of the most important scientists ever to live.

Centuries

One way to measure time is in centuries. A century is a period of 100 years. For example, the years 1 to 99 = 1st century, 100 to 199 = 2nd century, 200 to 299 = 3rd century, and so on.

In some places, Ibn al-Haytham is also known as Alhazen, which is the Latin form of his first name, al-Hasan.

This drawing is an artist's idea of what Ibn al-Haytham might have looked like.

Words to Know

SCHOLAR: A person who studies and has much knowledge

5

Growing Up in the Golden Age

Ibn al-Haytham was born in Basra in C.E. 965, during the Golden Age of Muslim civilization. Little is known about his childhood.

The Golden Age was a time of great learning in the Muslim world, which stretched from southern Spain to China. Men and women of different faiths and cultures studied science from earlier times and other cultures. They wanted to know about the world and to use this knowledge to improve people's lives.

That's a FACT! The calendar we use today begins with the year C.E. 1. The time before that counts backward. It ends in the year 1 B.C.E.

Yeni Cami mosque in Istanbul

The Golden Age

The Golden Age of Muslim civilization lasted from the 7th to the 13th century. During this time, people made amazing advances in science and created inventions we still use today. They invented early versions of guitars and the first hang glider. They even discovered coffee!

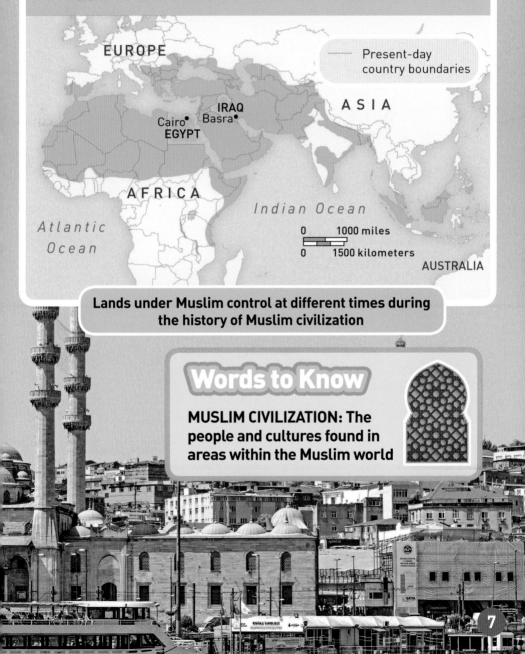

Present-day country boundaries

EUROPE

ASIA

IRAQ
Cairo•   Basra•
EGYPT

AFRICA

Indian Ocean

Atlantic Ocean

0   1000 miles
0   1500 kilometers

AUSTRALIA

Lands under Muslim control at different times during the history of Muslim civilization

Words to Know

MUSLIM CIVILIZATION: The people and cultures found in areas within the Muslim world

This illustration shows a public library during the Golden Age of Muslim civilization.

This clever clock was made during the Golden Age. It was powered by water and weights. Moving robotic figures told the time.

This was an exciting time for young students like Ibn al-Haytham. Highly trained scholars taught in schools. In Basra, the library held more than 15,000 books. Many of those books were great ancient works that had been translated into Arabic.

Students learned from scholars in many subjects. They talked about discoveries. They discussed and debated ideas. Ibn al-Haytham loved learning about everything and became a great scholar, too. Soon, people far beyond Basra knew about him.

Words to Know

TRANSLATE: To change words from one language into another

In His Time

When Ibn al-Haytham was growing up in Basra in the late 10th century, many things were different from the way they are today.

SCHOOL: Schools were mainly located in mosques (MOSKS), Muslim places of public worship. Both boys and girls started school at age six. Classroom time was very serious, with no laughing or joking allowed.

TRAVEL: People traveled by foot, on horse or camel, and by sea. They made maps and wrote about their travels so that they could share what they learned with others.

HEALTH: Hundreds of years before modern medicine, doctors in the Muslim world could treat all kinds of diseases, fix broken bones, and even do eye operations. They stitched up people after surgery using catgut, a cord made from animal intestines.

TOYS AND GAMES: People liked games that made them think. They played chess and did number puzzles. They built robotic toys that moved and made funny sounds so people could play tricks on one another.

TRADE: Traders traveled in large groups called caravans. They bought and sold goods across three continents.

Trouble in Egypt

Ibn al-Haytham was proud of his knowledge. He was so proud that he claimed he could control the flooding of Egypt's great Nile River by building a dam.

In His Own Words

"If I were given the opportunity, I would implement a solution to regulate the Nile flooding."

His words traveled to Egypt. The caliph (KAY-lif), al-Hakim (al-HA-kim), heard about Ibn al-Haytham's claim. Cairo, the capital of Egypt, is on the banks of the Nile River. The Nile flooded each year, causing great damage to crops. After the flooding, water levels were too low for more crops to grow.

Words to Know

CALIPH: An important Muslim leader, like a president

Nile River in Egypt

The caliph invited Ibn al-Haytham to Cairo and challenged him to control the flooding. Ibn al-Haytham accepted the challenge.

A thousand years after Ibn al-Haytham said a dam could help the Nile River, his idea came true. The powerful Aswan Dam controls the flooding in present-day Egypt.

He left to explore the Nile. Quickly he saw that he couldn't build a dam that would safely stop the flooding. If any dam could do that, he thought, the master builders of ancient Egypt would have built one long ago.

The Mad Caliph

Although al-Hakim was a great supporter of scholars and scientists, he was also known to be an unreasonable and cruel leader. He ordered many people to be harmed or killed for little or no reason. Because of this, many people called al-Hakim the Mad Caliph.

Ibn al-Haytham returned to Cairo to tell the caliph he had failed. He was afraid. He knew the caliph could be bad-tempered. Instead of punishing him, al-Hakim gave him a job as an expert adviser. But this job was no reward. Being near the caliph put Ibn al-Haytham in danger. To get away from the caliph, Ibn al-Haytham acted like he had gone mad. Al-Hakim put him under house arrest.

Words to Know

HOUSE ARREST: Keeping a person locked in a home as a form of punishment or as a way to protect other people

For more than ten years Ibn al-Haytham was held in Cairo. He could no longer talk with fellow scholars. He could no longer discuss and debate his ideas. He was alone.

But he did have time to think. He had time to read and learn. He had time to come up with new ideas that would change how people saw the world.

A Dazzling Discovery

The Golden Age of Muslim civilization was a time of great discovery. But there were still many things people didn't know. One big question was: How do people see?

For centuries, scholars had debated the ideas of ancient Greek thinkers. Some people believed that rays shoot out of our eyes, making things visible. Others thought that something comes into our eyes, allowing us to see. Ibn al-Haytham wondered if either of these ideas was correct.

i membranæ Volitant Simulacra per auras
patet quocunqué licet Caniuncta feruntur.

This picture illustrates the ancient Greeks' idea that people see because rays shoot out of their eyes.

Legend says that Ibn al-Haytham was sitting in a dark room one day. He noticed a bright light shining on the wall. He looked closer. It wasn't just a beam of light. It was an image of objects outside his room. But they were upside down. How was any of this possible?

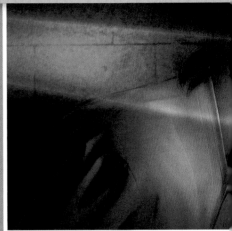

Ibn al-Haytham began to search for answers. The light was coming through a tiny hole in the wall. He blocked the hole with his hand. The image disappeared. He took his hand away. The image came back.

Suddenly, he understood. Light bounced off the objects outside, traveled through the hole, and made the image. He thought the opening at the front of an eye must do the same thing. Rays don't shoot out of an eye. Light comes in, just like the light coming in through the hole in the wall! This dark room was like an eye. That's how people see!

The Dark Room

In Ibn al-Haytham's time, many scholars simply believed that ideas from the past were true. They did not question what they read. They didn't think old ideas needed to be tested.

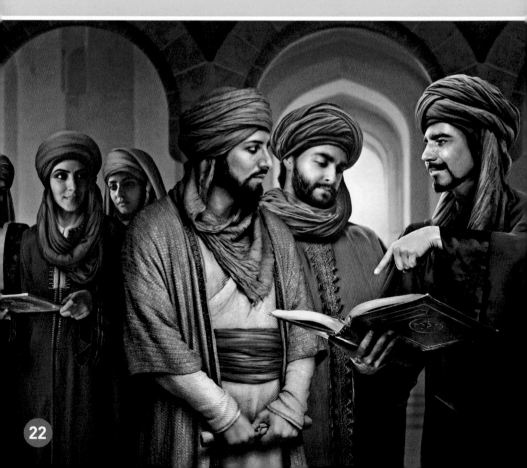

In His Own Words

"If learning the truth is the scientist's goal … then he must make himself the enemy of all that he reads."

Ibn al-Haytham disagreed. He wanted to test the old ideas, especially those about how people see. He wanted to prove which idea was correct. He also had new evidence from the light in the dark room. So he decided to start testing.

Ibn al-Haytham gathered supplies. He built a small box. A sheet of thin paper made up one side of the box. Across from the paper side was a small hole.

Next, he placed three lit candles outside the box in front of the hole. Then he looked at the sheet of paper.

The Camera Obscura

Ibn al-Haytham's box came to be known as the camera obscura. *Camera* is the Latin word for "room." *Obscura* means "dark." Experimenting with the box, he discovered that a smaller hole created clearer images. This idea led to the modern-day camera.

He saw an upside-down image of the three lit candles. The light from the flames was bouncing off of the candles, traveling through the hole, and making the image. The results were the same as what he had seen in his room. This proved that his idea of how we see was correct.

Light and Vision

Ibn al-Haytham kept testing. He started to have new ideas about light and how we see. Each test showed him new information.

In one test, he observed that the dots of light he saw always lined up perfectly with the beam of light coming in through a pinhole. He concluded that light travels in straight lines.

Words to Know

OBSERVE: To watch carefully as a way to learn something

CONCLUDE: To decide something after careful thought or based on evidence

He also noticed that light coming from different sources never got mixed up as it passed through the pinhole. This gave him more proof that light travels in straight lines. It helped explain why we see exactly what's around us.

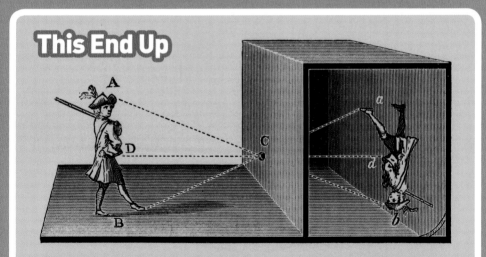

This End Up

Ibn al-Haytham concluded that light travels in straight lines. This diagram shows why objects in the images he saw were upside down. Light bounces off the top part of an object (point A). It travels in a straight line through the hole in the center of the box. The only place the light can land is down low (point *b*). Light travels in straight lines from every part of the object. This flips the whole image upside down. Since Ibn al-Haytham's time, we have learned that this happens in our eyes, too. But our brain knows to flip the image back, and we see the world right side up.

Ibn al-Haytham knew that light coming into the eye was just the first step. More had to happen in order for us to see. He wanted to know what that was. He studied what eyes are made of. He even found and named important parts of the eye.

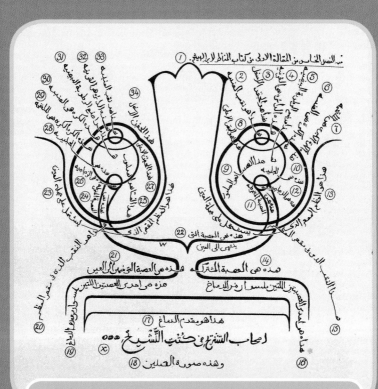

This diagram was based on Ibn al-Haytham's original drawing. It shows not only the parts of the eye but also how eyes are connected to the brain.

Ibn al-Haytham started to write a book about what he learned. In the *Book of Optics,* he explained how he tested his ideas. He wrote down every step of his experiments. He didn't just want to tell people what he had discovered. He wanted people to do the experiments themselves. He wanted them to see why his ideas were right.

This illustration appeared in the Latin edition of the *Book of Optics,* but it was not created by Ibn al-Haytham.

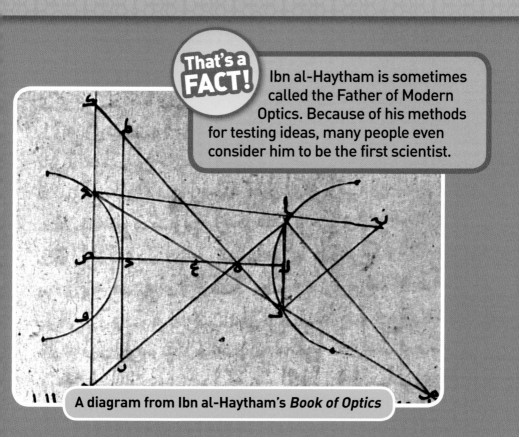

That's a FACT!

Ibn al-Haytham is sometimes called the Father of Modern Optics. Because of his methods for testing ideas, many people even consider him to be the first scientist.

A diagram from Ibn al-Haytham's *Book of Optics*

The *Book of Optics* encouraged people to ask questions about science. It showed them how to find the answers. It is the first example of the scientific method. Scientists still use this method today.

Words to Know

OPTICS: The science of light and vision

SCIENTIFIC METHOD: A way of using tests and observing the results to answer questions about science

6 COOL FACTS About Ibn al-Haytham

Ibn al-Haytham invented a clock powered by water. It may have been the first clock to give time in hours and minutes.

1

Alhazen crater

2 The Alhazen crater on the moon is named after Ibn al-Haytham. So is the asteroid 59239 Alhazen.

Ibn al-Haytham used math to show that moonlight is actually sunlight bouncing off of the moon's surface.

3

Ibn al-Haytham's work helped others create modern inventions such as cameras, movie projectors, eyeglasses, microscopes, and telescopes.

4

Ibn al-Haytham studied things people see that look different from the way they really are. These are called optical illusions. He said they are visual tricks played by the brain.

5

Ibn al-Haytham often used math to explain his ideas. The numbers he got weren't always exact, but modern scientists say he was on the right track.

6

Other New Ideas

Ibn al–Haytham also studied how light moves. He did tests using different types of lenses and mirrors. These tests taught him about reflection. Light reflects, or bounces back, when it hits a surface.

Other experiments with light taught Ibn al-Haytham about refraction. He learned that light refracts, or bends, when it moves through different materials.

Words to Know

REFLECTION: The bouncing back of light from a surface

REFRACTION: The bending of light as it passes through materials

Reflection

Refraction

Ibn al–Haytham also watched the sun, the moon, and the stars. This made him ask more questions. He did experiments to find the answers.

He wondered why the sky changes colors as the sun sets. He concluded that rays of sunlight refract as they pass through the air around Earth. When light bends, it separates into different colors.

He wondered why we can't see stars in the daytime. He concluded that the levels of brightness of the daytime sky and the stars are too similar. We see bright objects only when they are next to darker objects, such as the night sky.

He wondered why the moon appears
smaller when it's high in the sky
and larger when it's low in the sky.
He concluded that this is an
optical illusion.

Many scientists have tried to figure out why this happens. Although they have many ideas, no one has been able to find scientific proof. It's one of the oldest unsolved scientific puzzles remaining today.

A Lasting Legacy

Ibn al-Haytham made many important discoveries about light and vision. He did this while he was under house arrest. He continued his work after he was released.

C.E. 965	Around 1010	1010–1021
Born in Basra	**Placed under house arrest**	**Makes important discoveries about light and vision**

Ibn al-Haytham's Books

Ibn al-Haytham wrote at least 96 books. Only 55 are still around today. Many of his books are about light. They tell about his studies of the moon, stars, rainbows, mirrors, shadows, and the sun. His most famous book is the *Book of Optics.*

As a free man, he also taught and wrote. Around 1027 he finished the *Book of Optics.* He wrote many other books as well. In 1039, he died in Cairo. He was 74 years old.

1021

Released from
house arrest

Around 1027

Finishes the
Book of Optics

1039

Dies in Cairo
at age 74

For a time, Ibn al-Haytham's work seemed to be forgotten. Then in the early 12th century, his books were translated into Latin. Because more people knew Latin than Arabic, more scientists and scholars could study his work.

NAME: Roger Bacon
LIVED: 1220–1292
STUDIED: Bacon used the scientific method to study light. He told other scientists to test their ideas and observe the results, too.

NAME: Kamal al-Din al-Farisi
LIVED: 1267–1319
STUDIED: Al-Farisi studied Ibn al-Haytham's work on refraction. He then did tests with glass jars full of water to find out how rainbows are made.

NAME: Johannes Kepler

LIVED: 1571–1630

STUDIED: Kepler discovered how planets move around the sun. He also studied Ibn al-Haytham's work on optics. He even corrected some of Ibn al-Haytham's mistakes.

NAME: Isaac Newton

LIVED: 1643–1727

STUDIED: Newton studied Ibn al-Haytham's ideas about forces. He came up with new ideas about how gravity and motion work.

Over the centuries, many great thinkers learned from Ibn al-Haytham, just as he learned from ancient scholars who came before him.

QUIZ WHIZ

See how many questions you can get right!
Answers are at the bottom of page 45.

1

Where was Ibn al-Haytham born?

A. Greece
B. Cairo
C. Basra
D. Egypt

2

Ibn al-Haytham lived during the _____ of Muslim civilization.

A. Bronze Age
B. Silver Age
C. Iron Age
D. Golden Age

What does *camera obscura* mean?

A. Photograph
B. Dark room
C. Light ray
D. Pinhole

3

4

Ibn al-Haytham claimed he could control the _____ of the Nile River.

A. flowing
B. flooding
C. drying up
D. saltiness

5

What did Ibn al-Haytham study while under house arrest?

A. Light and vision
B. Hearing and sound
C. Smell and odor
D. Touch and feel

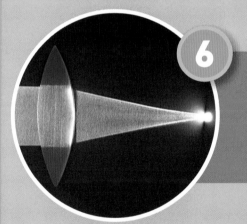

6

Ibn al-Haytham learned that light travels in _____.

A. refraction
B. straight lines
C. reflection
D. optical illusions

7

Who came up with new ideas by studying Ibn al-Haytham's work?

A. Kamal al-Din al-Farisi
B. Johannes Kepler
C. Isaac Newton
D. All of the above

Glossary

CALIPH: An important Muslim leader, like a president

MUSLIM CIVILIZATION: The people and cultures found in areas within the Muslim world

OBSERVE: To watch carefully as a way to learn something

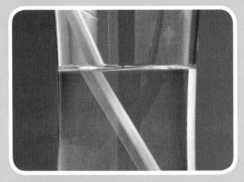

REFRACTION: The bending of light as it passes through materials

SCHOLAR: A person who studies and has much knowledge

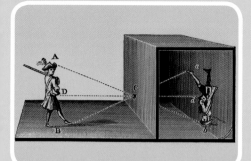

CONCLUDE: To decide something after careful thought or based on evidence

HOUSE ARREST: Keeping a person locked in a home as a form of punishment or as a way to protect other people

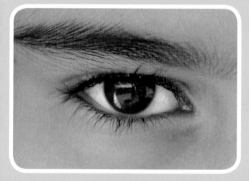

OPTICS: The science of light and vision

REFLECTION: The bouncing back of light from a surface

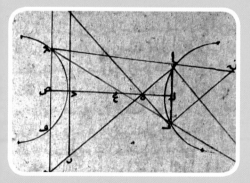

SCIENTIFIC METHOD: A way of using tests and observing the results to answer questions about science

TRANSLATE: To change words from one language into another

Index

Boldface indicates illustrations.